CHINESE
SPRING FESTIVAL

Ming Tsow

Photographs by Geoff Howard

Evans Brothers Limited

Everyone is happy when the winter is over and spring arrives. Chinese people celebrate this time of year with a Spring Festival. It is also known as the Chinese New Year. Everyone says goodbye to the old year and welcomes the chance to make a fresh start.

The Chinese New Year takes place between 21 January and 20 February. The exact date changes from year to year. It is fixed using a Chinese lunar calendar in which each month begins with the new moon.

In the Chinese calendar every year is named after an animal. They are Rat, Ox, Tiger, Rabbit, Dragon, Snake, Horse, Ram, Monkey, Rooster, Dog and Pig. The chart on page 2 shows the different animals and which years are named after them. Do you know which animal's year you were born in?

For Mei Fong and her brother Pak Wei the Spring Festival means celebrations at home and school as well as in China Town. The first sign at home is that Mum gives the house a good clean. By sweeping away the dust and dirt the family hope to get rid of the misfortunes of the past year. Mum pays special respect to the god of the household. He is supposed to make a yearly report on the family's behaviour to the Jade Emperor, the chief god.

At school Mei Fong and Pak Wei are practising for a display to celebrate the Chinese New Year. There will be singing, dancing and even some martial arts!

Mum and Dad go shopping to stock up for the
celebrations. They buy food to last from New Year's Eve
right through the New Year. In the old days people used to
celebrate for fifteen days. Now the festival usually lasts for
three days.

Every family likes to have special flowers and fruits for the New Year. They are supposed to bring prosperity and good fortune. Dad has bought some peach blossom. The pretty pink flowers are supposed to bring long life.

Mum has bought a kumquat plant. The kumquat tree has little golden fruits. The Chinese characters for this plant sound the same as the words for 'gold' and 'good luck'.

Mei Fong and Pak Wei can hardly wait for New Year's
Eve. This is a very important day. Relatives and friends
are invited to join in a happy reunion over a delicious
meal. Dad spends hours in the kitchen preparing the food.

Before the food is laid on the table Dad offers it to the gods of the Earth, wealth and heaven. He also pays respect to the family ancestors. Many Chinese people believe that the spirits of their dead ancestors live on and they treat them with great honour.

Dad also offers wine and paper money. The money is burnt in a candle flame. The family hopes that these offerings will please the gods.

Dad has proved himself to be a marvellous cook again!
There are stir-fried prawns, white chicken, roast pork,
steamed fish, braised mushroom and lettuce. There is also
a vegetarian dish that is only eaten on New Year's Eve.
One of the ingredients is a special seaweed called 'fat
choi'. In Chinese 'fat choi' also means prosperity.

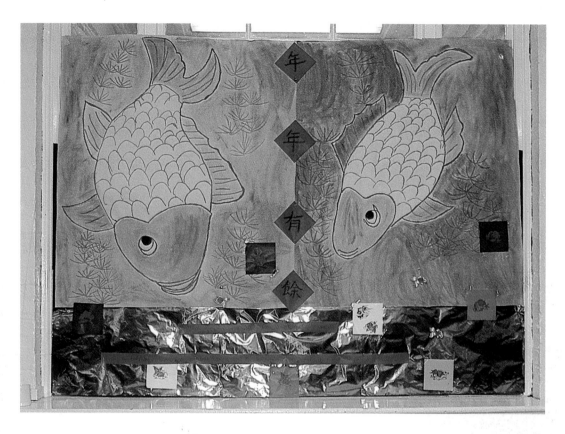

No New Year's meal would be complete without fish. At school, Mei Fong and her classmates have made a big painting of a fish. They have decorated it with New Year greetings, 'May there be abundance every year'. The Chinese character for 'abundance' sounds the same as 'fish'. The Chinese New Year is full of symbols of good wishes to get it off to a good start.

It's New Year's Day at last! Mum, Dad, Mei Fong and Pak Wei all have new clothes to wear. Mei Fong has a red and gold jacket made of padded silk. Her grandmother has sent it all the way from Hong Kong.

Mei Fong and Pak Wei wish Mum and Dad all the best for the year to come: 'Sun Nean Fai lok'. This means 'Happy New Year'. They then say 'Kung Hey Fat Choi', which means 'May prosperity be with you!'

Mum and Dad give Mei Fong and Pak Wei their traditional New Year's gift of 'lai see' (lucky money). 'Lai see' always comes in red and gold envelopes. Red is an important colour for Chinese festivals and celebrations, weddings and birthdays. Pak Wei can't resist taking the money out of his envelope straight away.

In China Town everyone has been busily preparing for the festival. There is fresh red and gold paint everywhere. The streets are decorated with banners, lanterns and streamers.

Mei Fong and Pak Wei are very lucky. They have
found a good place to watch from, on the top floor
of their uncle's shop. They can see everything going
on in the street below.

There are all sorts of things to look at: Chinese opera, comedy sketches, singing, acrobats and martial arts. The streets are full of people who have come to watch.

The best performance of them all is the fantastic lion dance. Pak Wei particularly wants to see it. He is going to take part in the school's lion dance in a few day's time.

It is a fabulous lion in red and gold with piercing black eyes. Lions are supposed to be brave and fearless. This lion is full of energy and movement.

Inside the lion there are two men. They make it prance
and whirl about.

Shopkeepers hang out 'lai see', lettuce leaves and other gifts for the lion to catch. The lettuce leaves stand for a new life.

The lion dances around and leaps up into the air to catch the 'lai see'.

One shopkeeper has put some food out in the street. For one moment Mei Fong thinks the lion is going to gobble up the table as well!

During the lion dance the street is filled with noise from firecrackers, drums and clashing cymbals.

Mum and Dad are expecting visitors in the afternoon and so the family leaves the China Town celebrations to go home. Mum and Dad lay out a variety of New Year delicacies for their guests.

There is a little tray full of delicious candied fruits and chocolates. These stand for peace and sweetness in the New Year. They come with a greetings card which says, 'May your house be full of gold and jade.'

20

On the table there are also some nuts and red and black melon seeds. These stand for wealth and prosperity.

Mei Fong is particularly looking forward to the special New Year cakes. The cake is in the middle of the back row called 'Nin Ko'. In Chinese 'Nin Ko' also means progress and improvement throughout the year.

A few days later Mum and Dad and other parents come to see the New Year celebrations at school. The hall is decorated with banners, streamers and posters.

Mei Fong has the job of introducing the programme in Cantonese and English. One of the performances is a display of Chinese song and dance.

The whole infants' class perform a nursery rhyme in
Chinese without making a single mistake! Here you can
see them pretending to be rabbits.

24

Pak Wei enjoys the singing, the dancing and the martial arts but secretly he thinks the lion dance is the best of all!

The New Year has arrived, the Spring Festival is over. It is time to settle into another year.

Crispy mo fa

Ingredients:
200g / 8oz plain flour
100g / 4oz lard
4 eggs
vegetable oil for frying
salt

Mix the lard and the flour with half a teaspoon of salt in a bowl. When the mixture becomes lumpy, whip the eggs and pour them into a well in the mixture. Knead the mixture for about 15 minutes. Then roll it flat with a rolling pin. Cut small rectangular pieces of about 4cm long and 2cm wide with a slit down the middle. Then turn them inside out. Deep fry in vegetable oil.

Published by Evans Brothers Limited
2A Portman Mansions
Chiltern Street
London W1M 1LE

First published in Great Britain in 1988 by
Hamish Hamilton Children's Books

© Ming Tsow (text) 1988
© Geoff Howard (photographs) 1988
© Tony Garrett (illustration) 1988
Design by Tony Garrett

Reprinted 1992

ISBN 0 237 60137 0

Printed in Hong Kong by Wing King Tong Co., Ltd.